A few years ago, I set out to find the "bottom line" when it came to finances in the kingdom. I needed to know how God viewed money, and how He felt I should be dealing with it. I prayed to the Lord that He would send me the wisdom I needed to get out of my rut. Things were tough back then. We had hit an air pocket in our financial life and I was trying to patch the leaks in our money boat. I was on a quest to right the "wrongs" in my thinking.

Where does one turn to find out the truth about finances? Advice abounds from everywhere. Everybody has something to say about it. We hear the world's wisdom on finances every day—whether we want to or not. I urge you to consider the source.

Recent events around the world have caused us all to gasp. The world as we knew it changed. Companies that we never thought would go bankrupt did just that. Whole countries have fallen, and their remedy to make it all better is to incur more debt. It is quite clear that very few saw this meltdown coming, and even fewer know how to fix it. That is the best the world has to offer—and there has to be a better way.

A short time after I set out to find the truth on finances, something wonderful happened. The truth found me. It walked in right through the front door of my house and sat on my couch. It was in the hand of a man. It was the Word of God. Yes, the Bible. Who was this man who was sent to me as an answer to my prayers and my pleading for financial wisdom? Johan du Toit. Advice comes in its purest form when it can be pointed to in the Bible, and that is exactly what Johan did. Everything I needed to know about my wealth, prosperity, and finances was in that Bible in his hand. It was the same Bible as the dusty old one on my bookshelf. He summed it up so eloquently that evening that I have never forgotten the words he used. He said, "You don't pray for money. The way you get money is by giving money." He then smiled and even let out a little chuckle. A childlike grin appeared on his face, and I have now come to realize why. It was because this huge life-changing revelation was almost embarrassingly too simple. Even I could understand it. However, the challenge is not in understanding the concept. The challenge lies in following it in obedience. I made up my mind that I was going to do what I heard, no matter what. I urge you to do the same. My life has not been the same since.

The Word has something to say about the many blessings and pitfalls we may encounter in our lives concerning finances. It is crucial for us to know about things such as pride in our giving, letting money work for you (instead of you working for money), unleashing the power of money, preparing yourself to give, giving with the right attitude, and knowing the purpose and balance of wealth. Fortunately for all of us, Johan has committed to further illustrate these key biblical points so that we may prosper abundantly, and come to know God as the *God of More Than Enough*. He delivers them to us in his usual courageous manner, devoid of any compromise or concern for what our fellow man may think. That alone makes him stand out in a crowd, and certainly a rarity to behold!

—Tony Bruccoleri
Church Member and Businessman
Canada

I have known pastor Johan for almost eighteen years now and every ministry he was involved in during this time has prospered financially. With this book he shares the powerful principles and secrets of God's economy that have brought so much success to his ministry with us in a very simple way. This book provides ministers of the gospel with a valuable tool to teach their churches sound biblical principles about financial giving. It also provides every Christian with much needed biblical guidance on how to give to God's work so that a bountiful harvest can be reaped. I highly recommend this book to every Christian.

—Pastor Willie Smit
Leopoldsburg, Belgium

God needs us to prosper. If we, the body of Christ, are to finance the End Time harvest, we will have to prosper supernaturally. This can be done by continuing to do what we know to do: give our tithes and offerings and receiving a special revelation of the unlimited and unconditional goodness of God. Why does God heal us? Because He is good. Why does He answer our prayers? Because He is good. Why does He prosper us? Because He is good. Why does He bless us? Because He is good and His goodness endures forever.

Your understanding of God's love and goodness for you will

directly affect your faith in God's abundance. You may be in need right now, but as you discover how much God loves you, faith will leap in your heart and blessing will come your way!

For thousands of years, the Lord had one big dream: that we might inherit the blessing of Abraham. This was done through the sacrifice of our Lord and Savior Jesus Christ. Now we can taste His blessings. God wants us to live from blessing to blessing.

In Proverbs 10:22, King Solomon gives us a secret about the blessing. It says, "The blessing of the LORD makes one rich, and He adds no sorrow with it." Solomon is very clear in this verse. The blessing has power. The blessing is not just a gift of God to be enjoyed, but it is also the power of God to be used. Using the blessing He gives us makes us rich. It empowers us with the resources necessary to live a carefree life and to advance the kingdom of God on earth.

The blessing is powerful. Once it has been spoken, it cannot be broken by men. It has power in itself. When Isaac blessed Jacob believing it was Esau, he could not take back the blessing because it was already spoken. God has blessed us with every spiritual blessing in heavenly places in Christ Jesus. (See Ephesians 1:3.) You are blessed. No one can break this. It has been spoken.

By reading this book, you will begin a wonderful experience. You are going to transform your mind from religious thinking to God's thinking about giving. If you are to undergo a life-changing experience, you will need to receive these principles, participate in them, and apply them to your life. These fifty-two chapters each contain one secret of the blessing of giving. They are excellent to prepare your heart for your tithes and offerings. They follow the principles of learning and revelation given in Isaiah 28:10 (NLT), "He tells us everything over and over—one line at a time, one line at a time, a little here, and a little there!" This is how this book works, too. It reveals one secret at the time, one principle at the time.

Giving to others brings indescribable pleasure. There is an inward joy when we reach out to help others—how much more it is when we give to God and His kingdom! When you give first, your own personal needs are being taken care of by the Lord.

Giving is *Christianity in action*. Yet, there are people who give with the wrong motives. Some give just to get something in return. Others give out of fear and not out of faith and love. Still others fail to honor their local church in their giving, but this does not have to be the case in your life. By applying the principles in this book you will learn to give the right way and experience the blessing of the Lord upon your life.

We gain by giving because giving attracts financial miracles. When we give to the kingdom of God, it will be given back to us (Luke 6:38). It is God's antidote for greed; it is God's way to channel His financial blessings to our lives, "Give freely and become more wealthy; be stingy and lose everything. The generous will prosper; those who refresh others will themselves be refreshed" (Prov. 11:24–25).

For every person, the Lord has a purpose. And that purpose is that you eventually become a blessing to others. As you learn the secrets of the blessing of giving, you will become a channel of the blessings that flow from God's heart to others.

Those who know Pastor Johan du Toit know that he lives what he teaches. Visiting his church is one of the most exciting experiences I have when I travel in Canada. The blessing is overwhelming; the atmosphere overtakes everyone, young and old. You can almost touch it. It is quite hard to describe.

It is the overflow of God's blessing that makes us rich and He adds no sorrow with it. Abundance, joy, and happiness are the fruits of the blessing. The members of Living Water Fellowship live it because, over the years, they have applied the secrets of Pastor Johan's book in their daily lives. Some truths cannot just be taught, they must be caught. Grab each secret this book reveals. Take hold of its truths and be changed by them.

—Pastor Donato Anzalone
Living Word Christian Center
Lugano, Switzerland

Impact. It means to have an immediate and strong effect on something or somebody. The Word of God has impact. There are men of God whose ability to "rightly divide the Word of Truth" makes an impact. You are holding in your hand a book that will have a strong and immediate effect on your life and on your finances. It has impact.

One of the core characteristics of the Christian life is to be a "giver." God is a Giver, Jesus gave all He had, and the believers in the early church gave abundantly, as well (Acts 2:45). These aspects are modeled for us in Scripture for good reason; we are to be givers.

Sadly, many believers today have misconceptions about what it means to "give." Happily, those misconceptions now can be removed from the heart and the mind through *Secrets of Financial Blessing*, pastor Johan du Toit's edifying and illuminating new devotional.

Pastor Johan provides thoughtful and practical insight to the truths about the purpose and principles of giving as revealed in the Bible. Within the pages of this book are keys to unlocking for the believer the true heart of giving and the benefits thereof. Scripture is filled with abundant riches for the believer, but never before has the concept of *giving* been so deftly and thoughtfully revealed. From tithing to sowing, prosperity to provision, investment and economy, everything you ever needed to know about the principles of giving are contained in these fifty-two, easy-to-read and understand devotionals.

Whether you are already a giver or you are seeking to understand the heart of giving, *Secrets of Financial Blessing* will increase your faith and finances, positioning you to impact the kingdom through God's blessing.

—Pastor Sylvia Wright
Nichols, New York

First things, first: whenever you read anything Pastor Johan has written, you must know that he lives what he teaches, preaches, and documents. To him, life and the ministry are not theory—they are lived and modeled.

Even before Johan left South Africa, he exhibited a passion for teaching. The following years in the mission field were revolutionary; his life tempered, challenged, and even broken. In His wisdom, God deemed these circumstances necessary to form an apostolic character in the life of this man God is now using to disciple others to be effective and living witnesses for His kingdom.

In the following weekly studies, Johan invites you to embark on a walk of faith and discovery with him. Yes, he invites you to realize that you are one of the few God is calling to pilgrim with Him. It will undoubtedly help you discover the truths necessary to prevail and much more—to be victorious and living life abundantly!

—Pastor Johan Carstens
Founder, MarketPlace Ministries
South Africa

SECRETS
of
FINANCIAL
BLESSING

SECRETS
of
FINANCIAL
BLESSING

JOHAN DU TOIT

CREATION HOUSE
A STRANG COMPANY

SECRETS OF FINANCIAL BLESSING by Johan du Toit
Published by Creation House
A Strang Company
600 Rinehart Road
Lake Mary, Florida 32746
www.strangbookgroup.com

Unless otherwise noted, all Scripture quotations are from the New King James Version of the Bible. Copyright © 1979, 1980, 1982 by Thomas Nelson, Inc., publishers. Used by permission.

Scripture quotations marked NLT are from the Holy Bible, New Living Translation, copyright © 1996. Used by permission of Tyndale House Publishers, Inc., Wheaton, IL 60189. All rights reserved.

Scripture quotations marked THE MESSAGE are from The Message: The Bible in Contemporary English, copyright © 1993, 1994, 1995, 1996, 2000, 2001, 2002. Used by permission of NavPress Publishing Group.

Scripture quotations marked NIV are from the Holy Bible, New International Version. Copyright © 1973, 1978, 1984, International Bible Society. Used by permission.

Design Director: Bill Johnson
Cover design by: Justin Evans

Copyright © 2010 by Johan du Toit
All rights reserved

Library of Congress Control Number: 2010922536
International Standard Book Number: 978-1-61638-163-9

First Edition

10 11 12 13 14 — 9 8 7 6 5 4 3 2 1
Printed in the United States of America

For believers.

For the church.

Hidden in the seed of the Word.

Contents

Preface

The Word Works

THE DEVOTIONALS IN this book endeavour to uncover some of the hidden truths about a painfully misunderstood area of life: finances. We have applied these thoughts in our church for years and found them to work. Although our church might be classified as a small congregation, the blessing that rests on us has been anything but. Our financial power is evidently not in proportion to our size, which demonstrates that God does not need numbers. He needs faith in His Word.

The blessing of our church is in relation to the blessing of its members. By embracing these proven principles in faith, you too can begin your journey on the high road of God's rich blessing on your life.

When Jesus told the devil in Matthew 4:4, "Man shall not live by bread alone, but by every word that proceeds from the mouth of God," He touched on a secret that most believers never explored. God created all things by the Word (Heb. 11:3) and He upholds all things by the Word (Heb. 1:3). A secret is a hidden truth, and God has a way of hiding truths in plain sight. These truths are keys to the abundant life, hidden *for* us—not *from* us.

In Isaiah 55:8–9, God speaks through the prophet and explains what is maybe man's greatest dilemma: the huge gap between His thoughts and ours; His ways and ours. This discrepancy has been our struggle since the Fall of Adam. Before man, created in God's image, fell from the highest position in all of creation, God *fellow-shiped* with him in person. Fellowship is "a company of equals," according to *Merriam-Webster*.[1] God could fellowship only with man in all of His Creation, for kind relates to kind.

Since God's thoughts and ways are so far above ours in our fallen state, we have been walking the low road where toil and struggle are our daily bread. Throughout history, we have been looking for methods and formulas to ease the pain of lack, while the key to blessing has been sitting right in front of our eyes.

> For as the rain comes down, and the snow from heaven, and do not return there, but water the earth, and make it bring forth and bud, that it may give seed to the sower and bread to the eater, so shall My word be that goes forth from My mouth; it shall not return to Me void, but it shall accomplish what I please, and it shall prosper in the thing for which I sent it.
>
> —Isaiah 55:10–11

The Word bridges the gap. Thus, if God's Word is true, we have no reason to doubt Him and no motivation to seek for other ways to make life work.

The New Testament opens with John the Baptist calling out, "Repent [change your thinking] for the kingdom of heaven is at hand" (Matt. 3:2, author's explanation). After His baptism, Jesus goes out and preaches the very same message. You cannot enter the kingdom with the thoughts, language, and culture of the dominion of darkness from which you have been redeemed, and you cannot embrace that which you do not know.

There are wonderful benefits available in God's kingdom waiting to be discovered. Before you can walk in the ways of the Lord, you have to change your thinking to line up with His. Every action is preceded by a thought; therefore, you must change your thinking before you can change your life, knowing that your attitudes and behaviour are the products of your thoughts.

The Word reveals to us the high thoughts of the Lord. Although it is not always possible to understand those thoughts, you can obey them in faith. Unfortunately, unrenewed minds tend to reject the thoughts of God because those thoughts do not make "sense," and that is how the keys to God's blessing remain hidden. You walk on God's high road by changing your thinking. Our minds, shaped by a fallen world and corrupt culture, are continually conditioned to walk the low road.

In the parable of the sower (Matt. 13), Jesus makes no mention of God, the Word, or anything spiritual. He simply tells an ordinary story about a normal, daily activity. When the disciples asked Him afterward about His parables, He pointed to hidden truths, "He answered and said to them, 'Because it has been given to you to know the mysteries of the kingdom of heaven'" (Matt. 13:11). Mysteries are hidden truths, and He says the ability to understand them was given to us that we might know them!

The multitudes that came to listen to Him only heard a story, but the disciples received the mystery hidden within the story. And so it is today. Some hear a story, some hear a sermon, but others hear a hidden truth, a key that unlocks the abundance of the kingdom of heaven.

Jesus then said something that I have read countless times, the meaning of which I missed for years: "For whoever has, to him more will be given, and he will have abundance; but whoever does not have, even what he has will be taken away from him" (Matt. 13:12). For whoever has *what?* Knowledge of the mystery; the hidden truth. The hidden truth in the parable of the sower is that the Word is the seed, with the potential to multiply and, like all seeds, the ability to produce without limit.

God spoke through Isaiah and declared that His Word would not return to Him void, but accomplish that for which He sent it. Potential is hidden ability, and the Word is packed with it! One could paraphrase Jesus' words to say, "To whoever has knowledge of this mystery, more will be given…and he will have abundance." The kingdom of God is a kingdom of abundance. Jesus also states in John 10:10 that He came to give life, and that more abundantly.

This book contains fifty-two of these life-giving secrets that unlock financial blessing, intended to be read when you prepare to give at your local church each week. I believe this message will do for you what it has done for us as you allow God's wisdom to shape your thinking about giving more and more in line with the teachings of His Word.

But he who received seed on the good ground is he who hears the word and understands it, who indeed bears fruit and produces: some a hundredfold, some sixty, some thirty.

—MATTHEW 13:23

WEEK 1
The Blessing of Giving

I have shown you in every way, by labouring like this, that you must support the weak. And remember the words of the Lord Jesus, that He said, "It is more blessed to give than to receive."
—Acts 20:35

ALTHOUGH PAUL WAS a missionary, he sometimes worked to support himself and those who traveled with him. We know that he was a tentmaker by trade (Acts 18:3). He did not work to build wealth for himself, but to help the weak and take care of himself and his helpers so they would not be a burden to the pagan Gentiles to which he ministered the gospel.

It is more blessed to give than to
receive…This is how faith is activated.

The culture of God's kingdom is unique in its attitude toward giving, with God setting the example. He always gives: He gave us His Son as ransom for our souls; He gives us grace every day; His mercies are new every morning; to every person on the earth He gives talents and skills to fulfill their lives and to earn a living; and He gives us peace and everlasting life, to name just a few of His blessings. A friend of mine once told me that if he were to give God a name, he would call Him, "Giver."

Paul showed by working as he did how we are to support the weak. I believe Paul also taught them how to build their faith and to embrace God's promises for their needs. But he also reached out to them in a practical way by working with his hands to support them.

The words, "it is more blessed to give than to receive," come from the Lord Jesus. Paul believed it and lived it, putting it into daily practice. This is how faith is activated. Do it because you believe, and expect His blessings in return.

WEEK 2
Value-Added Worship

"And blessed be God Most High, Who has delivered your enemies into your hand." And he gave him a tithe of all.
—GENESIS 14:20

THIS IS THE story of the first tithe ever given, and it happened more than four hundred years before the Law came into being. Without anybody telling him to do so, Abram gave a tithe to Melchizedek the high priest. Abraham, "the father of all who believe" (Rom. 4:11) had just returned from a mission to rescue his nephew Lot, who was taken captive after a raid on Sodom, where he lived. When he returned from his victory over the group of five kings that took Lot captive, Abraham gave a tithe of the spoils to the high priest.

Worship is a more meaningful experience by
honoring Him with one-tenth of your increase.

Have you ever wondered why he gave him the tithe? Because Melchizedek was the high priest and God's representative on earth. Abram gave him the tithe as a token of honor and gratitude for his victory. It also added value to his worship. This tithe was completely voluntary; there was no precedent, no law, no obligation; just an act of honor from a faithful heart.

Worship has real meaning when it is done in spirit and in truth, flowing from the heart. But, as the old saying goes, talk can be cheap, and a good way to add value to your worship is to put your money where your mouth is. We value money in today's world. And when you give money, you give value.

When worship means something to you, it will mean something to the Lord, as well. Make your worship a more meaningful experience by honoring Him with one-tenth of your increase.

WEEK 3
Sowing and Reaping

But this I say: He who sows sparingly will also reap sparingly, and he who sows bountifully will also reap bountifully.

—2 Corinthians 9:6

PAUL, TEACHING ON money matters in 2 Corinthians 8 and 9, uses familiar activities such as sowing and reaping to explain how God's economy works. His teaching is based on the plain common sense maxim that you cannot reap if you have not sown. You cannot sit and pray at the field and hope a crop will miraculously appear if you have not sown the seed into the soil. Farmers know that sowing seed is not throwing it away, because there will be a return. The principle of sowing and reaping determines that what you have sown will return to you multiplied, which is how farmers make a living.

> The principle of sowing and reaping determines that what you have sown will return to you multiplied...making fulfilling the Great Commission possible.

Another law of sowing and reaping is that you can only reap *what* you have sown. To produce a crop of beans, you must sow beans; kind produces kind. (See Genesis 1:11–12.) Apples produce apples, sheep produce sheep, and money produces money.

Why did Paul compare the giving of money to sowing and reaping? Because this is how the Lord provides money to finance the spreading of the gospel. If we were to give without receiving a return, we would be severely restricted in our efforts to take the gospel into all the world. Giving money and receiving back multiplied makes fulfilling the Great Commission possible.

Paul says that you reap in proportion to what you have sown; if you sow sparingly, you will reap sparingly. Conversely, if you sow abundantly, you will reap abundantly. At the end of the day, *you* determine the size of your financial crop!

WEEK 4
Sowing in Tears

Those who sow in tears shall reap in joy. He who continually goes forth weeping, bearing seed for sowing, shall doubtless come again with rejoicing, bringing his sheaves with him.

—Psalm 126:5–6

Sowing can be hard when you just do not have seed to sow. This Psalm paints a picture of such a difficult time. There is this farmer who has some wheat to sow, but there is also a need in his family. He struggles with the difficult decision to either use the seed to feed his family, in which case his immediate need will be taken care of, or sow the seed and have a crop to look forward to, in which case his family will have to go without for the time being.

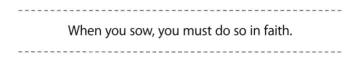

When you sow, you must do so in faith.

Hope and faith help him make that decision. He goes out and sows that seed, weeping, yet knowing that he will reap in joy. He looks past his circumstances and sees the day when the joy of the harvest will overshadow his present grief.

When you sow, you must do so in faith. God ordained for us to live by faith in Romans 1:17. If you cannot sow in faith, it is better not to sow at all.

In a time of drought and famine, Elijah called upon a widow to feed him with her last morsel of food (1 Kings 17:8–16). What otherwise looked unfair and selfish, resulted in activating a powerful principle that took care of this woman for the duration of the famine. When that widow sowed her last flour and oil by feeding it to the prophet, a crop of the same came pouring back into her life and did not stop until the famine was over.

It is not always possible to give out of abundance, but we can always give in faith, and that is what touches the heart of God and releases the flow of His provision.

WEEK 5
Firstfruits

Honor the LORD with your possessions, and with the firstfruits of all your increase; so your barns will be filled with plenty, and your vats will overflow with new wine.

—PROVERBS 3:9–10

WHATEVER IS AT the top of your list of priorities shows what is most important to you. People always ask the question, "Do you tithe on your gross or net income?" If you put God first, you give to Him before you give to the taxman or any other deductions from your income.

You honor God by giving Him the
firstfruits of your income or profit.

First things matter to God. In the Old Covenant era, God demanded the first of all increase: the firstborn of livestock belonged to Him (Exod. 13:12), and the first cutting of the wheat harvest and breads baked with the first ripe grain were to be presented to God as a wave offering (Lev. 23:17). Jesus tells us to seek *first* the kingdom of God. (See Matthew 6:33.)

You cannot honor God by giving Him second place or second best! You do so by giving Him the firstfruits of your income, whether it is your salary or profit. Some people "pay" their tithe after they have paid all their bills and took care of all their financial obligations, but too often there is no tithe or offering left to give to God after that.

You honor God by giving Him the firstfruits of your income or profit.

Don't merely *pay* your tithe—*honor* Him with it. According to King Solomon, God rewards honor with honor. Your barns will be filled with plenty and your vats will overflow—today's savings and investment accounts. The only working relationship we can have with God is one where He is always first in all things. It is a matter of honor.

WEEK 6
The Exchange

For it is written in the law of Moses, "You shall not muzzle an ox while it treads out the grain." Is it oxen God is concerned about? Or does He say it altogether for our sakes? For our sakes, no doubt, this is written, that he who plows should plow in hope, and he who threshes in hope should be partaker of his hope. If we have sown spiritual things for you, is it a great thing if we reap your material things?
—1 Corinthians 9:9–11

WHEN ISRAEL TOOK possession of the Promised Land, the Levites were not given any land because they were not allowed to do any work other than their priestly duties. The tithes of the people were their inheritance so that they could devote all of their time and energy to do God's work.

The minister sows "spiritual things" to the flock, but reaps "material things" from them.

In the text above, Paul likens ministers to oxen that plough the field. They work the field, which represents God's people. As the field provided for the oxen, ministers should not to be muzzled, but allowed to eat from the field on which they are working.

Today, in the New Testament era, our ministers stand in the place of the Levites as God's servants in the church. Although the *form* of ministry changed somewhat, the *principles* of supporting them remain.

Paul also explains that there is an exchange that takes place: the minister sows "spiritual things" to the flock, but reaps "material things" from them; a different application, but the same principle.

> Even so the Lord has commanded that those who preach the gospel should live from the gospel.
> —1 Corinthians 9:14

SECRETS OF FINANCIAL BLESSING

God's servants should be able to fulfil their duties with undivided attention. Generous giving will enable the church to take good care of the pastor with a salary that compares well with what he could earn in a secular occupation. When he can take good care of his family, he will be able to take good care of the flock.

What You Give and What You Keep

Now Jesus sat opposite the treasury and saw how the people put money into the treasury. And many who were rich put in much. Then one poor widow came and threw in two mites, which make a quadrans. So He called His disciples to Himself and said to them, "Assuredly, I say to you that this poor widow has put in more than all those who have given to the treasury; for they all put in out of their abundance, but she out of her poverty put in all that she had, her whole livelihood."
—MARK 12:41–44

W̲E̲ ̲D̲O̲ ̲N̲O̲T̲ always pay much attention to what poor widows do when we look for great examples of giving, but the Lord does. Jesus noticed how much this poor widow gave into the offering basket, and knew that she had nothing left after she gave her offering. He also saw that the many rich people that day gave much out of their abundance.

This poor widow impressed the Lord, not because of the amount she gave, but by her attitude and faith.

Both what we give and what we keep matter to God. While He never instructed us to give all that we have, this widow did so voluntary. We do not know what moved her to do so, but we do understand that she had to depend on God to provide for her.

During my years of ministry, I have noticed often how people gave in their need. Sometimes it hurt to see how they put all on the altar for the sake of the gospel, but I have also seen how things turned around for them as they were faithful to the Lord in small things and under difficult circumstances.

This poor widow impressed the Lord, not because of the amount she gave, but by her attitude and faith. Lack is never a good excuse *not* to give. Do all things in faith, in what you give and in what you keep.

WEEK 8
Giving, Not Getting, Makes You Rich

There is one who makes himself rich, yet has nothing; and one who makes himself poor, yet has great riches.

—Proverbs 13:7

Gᴏᴅ's ᴇᴄᴏɴᴏᴍʏ ᴏᴘᴇʀᴀᴛᴇꜱ on the principle of giving in faith. Conventional wisdom teaches that giving leaves you with less, but this is not how it works in the kingdom. The faith-challenged Christian is no different from the non-believer when it comes to giving, because it makes no sense to the carnal mind. Yet, the hoarding up of money is no guarantee for wealth. It can disappear faster than it came. It only takes one negative report for fortunes to be wiped off the computer screens of the world's markets. On the other hand, those who give faithfully and generously seem to have their needs met. They go through life without anxiety. God systematically provides for them as they continue to give. Why would He stop the flow to those who finance the operations of His kingdom?

Wealth has a God-given purpose!

How do you make yourself poor? Most would say by giving your money away. Yet the verse above says "one who makes himself poor has great riches." Giving, then, does not make you poor. This is one of God's hidden principles for blessing. Religion teaches people to believe that it is sinful to pursue riches, but what they do not realize is that you cannot fulfil the Great Commission to take the gospel to all nations without money. (See Matthew 28:19.) The gospel is free, but only to those who receive it; the bills are paid by those who bring the news. You cannot print Bibles and tracts, travel everywhere to preach the gospel, or feed the hungry, without money.

God made Abraham rich (Genesis 14:22–23) as part of His covenant with him. When the Israelites left Egypt as a nation of slaves, God placed riches in their hands because they had to build Him a tabernacle in the wilderness. (See Exodus 12:35–36.) Wealth has a God-given purpose! Abuse of money brings misery, but when it is spent for God's purposes, we can trust our Lord in faith to keep it flowing to and through us.

WEEK 9
Rich Fools

But God said to him, "Fool! This night your soul will be required of you; then whose will those things be which you have provided?"
—LUKE 12:20

THE PARABLE IN Luke 12:16–21 tells the story of a rich farmer who did very well for himself. He was so successful that he did not know what to do with all his wealth. Then he decided to enlarge his barns so that he could store it all. It was a good plan, but he made a mistake by thinking only of himself. God then spoke to him and told him that he would die that very night and that someone else, who did not work as hard as he did, would walk away with it.

Success is not solely the ability to gain wealth; success is also having the wisdom to spend wealth wisely.

This man did well and was very successful, yet God called him a fool. Everybody else probably saw him as a successful man. In reality, he was nothing but an ordinary fool. What you see is not always what you get! The only real success is to do the will of God, for "he who does the will of God abides forever" (1 John 2:17).

The man in this parable made the same mistake as Adam, namely to think only of eating and drinking and having a good time for himself, "For none of us lives to himself, and no one dies to himself." (Rom. 14:7).

Success is not solely the ability to gain wealth; success is also having the wisdom to spend wealth wisely. The farmer in Luke's parable made a mistake that cost him his eternal destiny, a much greater loss than all the wealth he could lose on earth. His focus was only on his own life, and how much enjoyment he could get for himself.

This mindset still deceives people today. Modern life can offer so much comfort that comfort easily begins to seem like a necessity. As a result, we can forget to make provision for eternity.

The *outward appearance* of success is a dangerous deception, especially if it comes at the expense of your eternal destiny. It doesn't matter what people think of you—just don't ever let God call you a fool!

WEEK 10
Investments That Disappear

Do not lay up for yourselves treasures on earth, where moth and rust destroy and where thieves break in and steal; but lay up for yourselves treasures in heaven, where neither moth nor rust destroys and where thieves do not break in and steal. For where your treasure is, there your heart will be also.

—Matthew 6:19–21

WE LIVE IN a time when we can see billions of dollars worth of investments disappear in a moment. The forces of fear and greed drive the fragile stock markets of our day. A single commodity, such as oil, has the potential to impact the price of everything else as it rises and falls. Your entire life's savings can disappear in a snap, leaving you with nothing.

Do not forget to prepare for eternity while
you have the opportunity to do so.

The harsh reality is that our world is troubled and delicate. Our financial systems, sophisticated as they are, offer no guarantee that our investments are safe.

Jesus reminds us of the brokenness of our world when He advises us not to lay up riches for ourselves where they can vanish or be destroyed. Life on earth is not all there is to life. Do not forget to prepare for eternity while you have the opportunity to do so. We live in two spheres at the same time, the natural and the spiritual, and we must be fruitful in both. There are the visible and the invisible, the present and future, the temporary and eternal; each of these is equally real.

Jesus says our treasure will be where our heart is. Remember—God's currency is people, not dollars. Invest in the good news that adds to God's treasure, and lay up for yourself riches that pay dividends throughout eternity.

WEEK 11
Cheerful Giving

So let each one give as he purposes in his heart, not grudgingly or of necessity; for God loves a cheerful giver.

—2 Corinthians 9:7

Giving for any cause is not something you should ever do on the spur of the moment or under pressure. We make our worst decisions when we are negative, when we feel guilty, or when we do not think about things first. You have been blessed with a free will, because the Lord wants to see that you serve Him out of love and not by force as a slave.

The joy of giving is your protection against manipulation. When you consider your offering, take some time to "purpose in your heart" regarding your gift. That does not mean it will always be a specific amount, but it will help you stay accurate according to God's will and to express your love for the Lord in a meaningful way.

When you give more than you can afford, whether out of guilt or presumption, your joy will soon turn into sorrow and that does not glorify the Lord. God loves a cheerful giver, not a guilty or manipulated one, so it is better not to give if you are going to do so grudgingly.

The joy of giving is your protection against manipulation.

What matters most to God is the attitude of your heart. He knows when you give cheerfully or of necessity, and whether you were inspired by your love for Him, or some other motivation.

> I want each of you to take plenty of time to think it over, and make up your own mind what you will give. That will protect you against sob stories and arm-twisting. God loves it when the giver delights in the giving.
>
> —2 Corinthians 9:7, The Message

Providing for the Lord?

Now it came to pass, afterward, that He went through every city and village, preaching and bringing the glad tidings of the kingdom of God. And the twelve were with Him, and certain women who had been healed of evil spirits and infirmities—Mary called Magdalene, out of whom had come seven demons, and Joanna the wife of Chuza, Herod's steward, and Susanna, and many others who provided for Him from their substance.

—LUKE 8:1–3

WHO WOULD EVER think of providing for the Lord! Isn't He supposed to be *our* Provider? Well, the Lord does need our help. Jesus went from city to city and village to village, preaching, teaching, and helping all who were in need. He traveled with twelve men, which is a large group to take care of. Every ministry has expenses, and Jesus' earthly ministry was no exception. In short, He needed someone to finance His ministry.

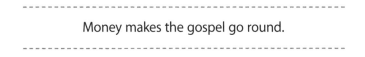

Money makes the gospel go round.

As a pastor and missionary who travels often, I know firsthand that taking the gospel around the world is a costly undertaking. You cannot go to an airline and demand a ticket just because it is for the gospel, nor can you stay in a hotel, print literature, or even buy Bibles without money.

Every dollar given to the work of the Lord is for a missionary. Money makes the gospel go round, whether it is around the block or around the globe.

Before the women in Luke 8 met Jesus, they were bound by the devil. Their lives changed when they met Him and they knew He could do the same for others. They understood how important it is to keep Him going and therefore provided for Him, and so should we. Let's help Him reach, with the good news of the gospel, those who are trapped. He still cares and He can help. Material money can do spiritual work.

WEEK 13
The Winds and Clouds of Circumstances

He who observes the wind will not sow, and he who regards the clouds will not reap.

—ECCLESIASTES 11:4

FARMERS NEVER KNOW what kind of year it will be when it is time to put their seed into the ground. They sow believing that the rain will fall at the right time and that circumstances will be ideal for a good crop to be harvested. They do not wait for the wind to blow from the right direction or for the clouds to promise rain. Sowing happens with faith, not when circumstances seem ideal.

It is God who takes care of us, not our money.

Pastors often get to hear the most creative excuses why people cannot give, but they do not need to know because we give to the Lord, not our pastor. The simple truth is that you cannot expect a harvest if you did not sow. If you have been watching the wind and the clouds of your circumstances, you probably missed some good opportunities to sow into a bountiful harvest.

We do not give because we have abundance, or because we have no financial threats looming on the horizon; we do not give because all of our needs are met and bills are paid—we give because we honor the Lord and believe in the cause of His kingdom.

When we put our money in the offering basket, we should be sowing in faith like a good farmer and be doing so without paying attention to the clouds and winds of circumstances.

Without the farmer's faith, there would not be enough food in the world. After all, it is God who takes care of us, not our money. The Lord needs your faith to take the gospel message to the lost and to have a church where people can be restored, equipped, and sent out as ambassadors of His kingdom.

WEEK 14
When Not to Give

Therefore if you bring your gift to the altar, and there remember that your brother has something against you, leave your gift there before the altar, and go your way. First be reconciled to your brother, and then come and offer your gift.

—MATTHEW 5:23–24

I T IS NOT always right to give. Remember, God is not after your money, but your heart. And your heart should not only be pure toward Him, but also with regard to others. Our love for God runs through our love for other people. You cannot love God and not love the people that He loves.

> If someone says, "I love God," and hates his brother, he is a liar; for he who does not love his brother whom he has seen, how can he love God whom he has not seen?
>
> —1 JOHN 4:20

God is not moved by your money, but by your faith and love. It is so easy to become proud of your giving without considering the condition of your heart. Jesus commands us not to bring offerings to the altar if we have unresolved issues with fellow believers. He says to leave our gift there and then go and reconcile first before giving it. This may not be common practice in Christianity, yet it is the Lord's command in Matthew 5. Money is only clean if it comes from a clean heart.

There is no point in bringing a gift to the altar if it does not come from a pure heart. The value of your gift is determined by the motivation of your heart, not the amount.

- -

God is not moved by your money,
but by your faith and love.

- -

The hard part of this command is that it is up to you to be reconciled to your brother if you know he has something against you, not the other way around. The Lord values unity in His household above money. There is greater power in the unity of the brethren than in the money we can raise. Our love for one another that flows from the heart of the giver sanctifies the offering and adds to it a pleasing aroma from the Lord.

God Calculates, and So Should We

Will a man rob God? Yet you have robbed Me! But you say, "In what way have we robbed You?" In tithes and offerings.

—MALACHI 3:8

IN A SERMON my grandparent's pastor once preached when I was just a teenager, he said that God counts and calculates and that numbers and figures are important to Him. He said God does math and we should, too, if we want to walk in step with Him. Have you noticed how often the Bible mentions numbers and figures?

Wonderful promises are attached to faithful giving.

Jesus knew that he had to feed *five thousand* men with *five* loaves and *two* fish, and that they picked up *twelve* baskets of leftovers afterward. He counted *two* coins that the poor widow put into the offering and knew that she had *nothing* left after that. When the disciples went fishing after Jesus rose from the dead, He knew that they had caught nothing. Then He told them to cast their nets on the right side of the boat and they caught *153* large fish.

Jesus knew He healed *ten* lepers, but only *one* came back to thank Him. He knew how much He and Peter owed on their taxes and provided a gold coin in the mouth of a fish to pay for it. God knows how much a tenth of your income is and He looks to see if you will add a love offering on top of it. But, be clear—your tithe is not an offering, it is just giving back the firstfruits to the Lord from what He entrusted to you in stewardship of His provision. After that, your offering is what you give from your heart to express your love for Him.

The Lord says that we rob Him if we do not give tithes *and* offerings. *Rob* is a strong word that means to take something by force. It is not smart to rob the One that you expect to bless you! Wonderful promises are attached to faithful giving. God says He will rebuke the devourer on our behalf—those unexpected expenses that eat away your money as fast as it comes in. He even invites us to try Him in this in Malachi 3:10.

Can you afford to rob the Lord?

WEEK 16
A Very Powerful Principle

Don't pick on people, jump on their failures, criticize their faults—unless, of course, you want the same treatment. Don't condemn those who are down; that hardness can boomerang. Be easy on people; you'll find life a lot easier. Give away your life; you'll find life given back, but not merely given back—given back with bonus and blessing. Giving, not getting, is the way. Generosity begets generosity.
—LUKE 6:37–38, THE MESSAGE

THE DEFAULT OF life in our fallen world is brokenness and decay, but God's principles release blessing when activated by acts of faith.

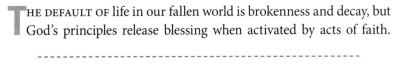

You always reap more than you have sown.

The principle of giving away the very thing that you need seems to be the greatest of all spiritual laws. Even God used that principle when He gave His only begotten Son to die for our sins, then gained us all. By giving His Son, He received many sons through the Lord Jesus Christ. (See Hebrews 2:10.)

Giving what you need is like sowing seed—if you want wheat, you have to sow wheat; if you want corn, you must sow corn. The good news is that you always reap more than you have sown. In the verses above, we see how it works: if you do not sow judgment, you will not reap judgment; if you sow forgiveness, you will reap forgiveness. You have to give what you need!

Apply this principle to your need. Sow your seed *in faith,* and see the fruit come in after a season or two.

George Boldt was the son of poor Prussian immigrants who moved to the United States in the 1860's. Unable to speak English, he started working as a waiter, but worked himself up to become a hotel magnate with an empire of hotels. When asked the reason for his success, he answered simply, "I have always tried to be generous."[1]

What you give is what you get. Generosity begets generosity. Do not hold on to your seed!

Tithing in the New Testament

Woe to you, scribes and Pharisees, hypocrites! For you pay tithe of mint and anise and cummin, and have neglected the weightier matters of the law: justice and mercy and faith. These you ought to have done, without leaving the others undone.

—MATTHEW 23:23

WELL, IS TITHING in the New Testament or isn't it? Those who have a hard time with giving argue that it isn't, but it is. Jesus Himself referred to it. I believe the reason why it is not often mentioned in the New Testament is that it was already a very well established practice at the time.

A pure heart is known…by justice, mercy, and faith.

In the verse above, Jesus was having a conversation with the religious leaders of His day. They were good at polishing the outside of the cup while leaving the inside dirty, and so they tithed to be seen and admired by the people. Jesus did not rebuke them for tithing, but for neglecting the issues of the heart.

These Pharisees tithed on all their increase to hold up the outward appearance of godliness, but they ignored justice, mercy, and faith, by which a pure heart is known. They were only concerned about the opinions of people.

Tithing is in the New Testament, and, as in the Old Testament, it still opens the windows of heaven so that blessing can be poured out to God's people. The Lord never recalled anything concerning tithing.

As a believer, you *ought* to tithe, but be careful not to neglect the weightier matters of justice, mercy, and faith.

God says to bring all the tithes into the storehouse so that there will be food in His house. (See Malachi 3:10.) The food is not for Him, of course, but for us. The storehouse is your local church where you are fed spiritually. Every household has expenses and it is no different with the local church. You keep the pantry of your spiritual house filled with good things by bringing your tithes and offerings into it. If you take care of your spiritual household, it will take good care of you.

WEEK 18
Profitable Investments

He who has pity on the poor lends to the LORD, And He will pay back what he has given.

—PROVERBS 19:17

A s WE READ the Bible, we see God's compassion for the poor running like a thread from beginning to end. Poverty is a curse that came upon humanity when Adam fell from God's blessing. Because of God's compassion on the poor, we know that poverty is not of Him. Time after time, when Israel drifted away from God, they stirred up His anger by neglecting the poor.

Will you be His hand extended?

Taking care of the poor is doing God's will. The first thing that Jesus came to do, as He announced His earthly ministry in Luke 4:18, was to bring good news to the poor. It is not God's will for people to be poor and to go without the necessities of life.

Giving to the poor, according to King Solomon, is lending to the Lord. And God always pays back—with interest—we have found.

My wife and I once received a call late one Monday evening from parents telling us that their children would have nothing to eat when they woke up the next morning. Our supermarkets are open around the clock, so we went and bought them some things to put on the table and to take to school for lunch. We also bought some things they would never buy themselves under those circumstances, like snacks and fruit juice. The following Monday, just a week later, God paid back the loan, with interest. For no reason at all, somebody gave us a check for exactly ten times the amount we spent on that family.

God's eye is on the poor to help. Will you be His hand extended? Will you be the bearer of good news to somebody in need? If you do so in faith, it will be one of the most satisfying experiences you will ever enjoy. Working with the Lord is an adventure!

WEEK 19
His Poverty, Our Riches

For you know the grace of our Lord Jesus Christ, that though He was rich, yet for your sakes He became poor, that you through His poverty might become rich.

—2 CORINTHIANS 8:9

ONE OF THE first curses that came on Adam after he fell in sin was lack. God sent him out of the garden of abundance to earn his living by the sweat of his brow in Genesis 3:19. But the first thing that Jesus mentioned regarding His earthly mission was to bring good news to the poor. Interestingly enough, His first miracle was a miracle of provision when He turned the water into wine. (See John 2.) This was not a miracle to turn a desperate situation around, but one to reveal God's goodness and kindness to man.

Contrary to religious belief, Jesus was not poor when He walked the earth. He traveled with twelve men, which calls for a generous budget. Judas carried the moneybag and stole from it all the time (John 12:6), which points to the fact that there was enough money to take care of their needs and sustain Judas's pilfering at the same time. With all of that going on, Jesus was never caught in a situation of lack. His Father always provided all of His needs. Twice, He fed a multitude from a handful of food, and ended up with more than when He started. Jesus paid His taxes and Peter's and provided breakfast for the disciples after He rose from the dead. When He was crucified, He wore such a special garment that the soldiers decided not to divide it among themselves, but rather cast lots to see who would have it. (See John 19:23–24.)

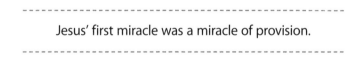

Jesus' first miracle was a miracle of provision.

When did Jesus become poor? On the cross, when they took His clothes and He hung there, naked. There, He became sin, poor and sick for us, taking the curse upon Himself that we might be free. (See 2 Corinthians 5:21; Isaiah 53:4.)

Some say His poverty and riches were spiritual, but a spiritually poor person cannot turn water into wine, heal the sick, raise the dead, or multiply food. On the cross, Christ also provided redemption from poverty!

Jesus gave His life to destroy the work of the devil, which includes poverty. This is the power of giving!

WEEK 20
The Riches of Liberality

Moreover, brethren, we make known to you the grace of God bestowed on the churches of Macedonia: that in a great trial of affliction the abundance of their joy and their deep poverty abounded in the riches of their liberality. For I bear witness that according to their ability, yes, and beyond their ability, they were freely willing, imploring us with much urgency that we would receive the gift and the fellowship of the ministering to the saints.

—2 CORINTHIANS 8:1–4

LTHOUGH THE CHURCHES in Macedonia were located in an area stricken by extreme poverty, it did not stop them from giving offerings to the churches in Jerusalem. Paul writes that they were in a great trial of affliction and in deep poverty, yet they freely gave beyond their ability. The apostle uses these faithful Christians as an example to challenge the wealthier Corinthians in their giving.

When God becomes your Provider, you can
freely give, even in a situation of lack.

In verse 1, Paul says that it is a *grace* that God bestowed on them. He then goes on to encourage Titus, as he prepares to receive the offering from the Corinthians, to "complete this grace in you as well" (v. 6). The Macedonian Christians, in their poverty, raised the bar and became an example to their more wealthy brothers in Corinth—and to us today.

Nobody asked the Macedonians to give money. No, they "implored" Paul "with much urgency" to receive it from them. They did not see it as an offering, but rather as "fellowship of the ministering to the saints." Their heart was to give to God's people.

When God becomes your Provider, you can freely give, even in a

SECRETS OF FINANCIAL BLESSING

situation of lack. That is the riches of liberality and a grace that can only come from God.

Grace empowers where the circumstances are contrary. With God, all things are possible!

WEEK 21
The Love of Money

But those who desire to be rich fall into temptation and a snare, and into many foolish and harmful lusts which drown men in destruction and perdition. For the love of money is a root of all kinds of evil, for which some have strayed from the faith in their greediness, and pierced themselves through with many sorrows.

—1 TIMOTHY 6:9–10

CARELESS READERS OF the Bible are quick to label money as something that is evil, but there is nothing wrong with money. God gives us the power to get wealth (Deuteronomy 8:18), therefore it is holy and should be treated as such. Everything that comes from Him is holy!

The purpose of money is to do God's will and
to establish His covenant on the earth.

The danger that Paul warns against is not money, but the love for money and the desire to be rich. It can move you to do some very unholy things, which ultimately means the abuse of a holy gift from the Lord. Human nature is vulnerable and capable of indescribable evil, whether you are rich or poor.

The purpose of money is to do God's will and to establish His covenant on the earth (Deuteronomy 8:18), and the purpose of the covenant is blessing. Money is a great servant in the kingdom of God, and capable of changing lives and helping to bring many to salvation and maturity in the Lord. But it also has the power to destroy just as many lives, as well as to separate people from a loving God.

Paul warns Timothy that the *love for* money is a root of all kinds of evil because it opens the door to all kinds of temptation, leads one into a snare, and in the end causes destruction. There is a difference between owning money or being owned by it; having

SECRETS OF FINANCIAL BLESSING

riches as a servant, or serving riches. Your heart will be where your treasure is.

As you consider your gift to the Lord, search your heart and see where your treasure is. Be guided by your love for *Him*, not the love for *money*.

WEEK 22
Sharing Your Blessings

When you gather the grapes of your vineyard, you shall not glean it afterward; it shall be for the stranger, the fatherless, and the widow.
—Deuteronomy 24:21

And when she rose up to glean, Boaz commanded his young men, saying, "Let her glean even among the sheaves, and do not reproach her. Also let grain from the bundles fall purposely for her; leave it that she may glean, and do not rebuke her."
—Ruth 2:15–16

WHAT YOU HAVE is never entirely yours to enjoy. God instructed Israel to leave some of their harvest for the stranger, the fatherless, and the widow, so that His goodness could reach them, also. Those who were unable to take care of themselves, for some reason, could benefit from His blessing on others.

Since those under the Old Covenant were not born again, they had the Law to guide them. It was a good law, but something better was to come in the New Testament, namely the law of love, which always goes the extra mile. Boaz was an Old Testament believer, but he went above and beyond the requirements of the Law when he told his workers to leave more than they usually did, to help Ruth.

God instructed Israel to leave some of their harvest
for the stranger, the fatherless, and the widow,
so that His goodness could reach them.

Jesus fulfilled the Law and gave us a new commandment that goes much further than the Ten Commandments of the Law of Moses:

> "And you shall love the LORD your God with all your heart, with all your soul, with all your mind, and with all your

strength." This is the first commandment. And the second, like it, is this: "You shall love your neighbor as yourself." There is no other commandment greater than these.

—MARK 12:30–31

Love shares because it cares.

WEEK 23
The Amazing Power of Money

Now while they were going, behold, some of the guard came into the city and reported to the chief priests all the things that had happened. When they had assembled with the elders and consulted together, they gave a large sum of money to the soldiers, saying, "Tell them, 'His disciples came at night and stole Him away while we slept.' And if this comes to the governor's ears, we will appease him and make you secure." So they took the money and did as they were instructed; and this saying is commonly reported among the Jews until this day.

—MATTHEW 28:11–15

THE GUARD THAT protected Jesus' grave experienced firsthand the most wonderful event of all time—the Resurrection of Jesus Christ. I cannot begin to imagine what it must have been like to witness that! It was the greatest moment in the history of the world, and the guards who saw it rushed to the chief priests to tell them what they had seen. Instead of believing it, though, they hardened their hearts and gave the soldiers a large sum of money to lie about it.

Your money has the power to bring life to others.

How anyone could ever lie about such an amazing event boggles the mind, yet that is what happened. The chief priests devised a lie, financed it with money, and sent it into the world where it is still widely believed two thousand years later. That is the power of money.

How different things could have been were these soldiers allowed to tell the truth, and if the priests turned to faith in Christ!

Your money has the power to bring life to others. You can finance the truth that sets people free and exposes the lies of the devil. Every dollar we give has this power.

SECRETS OF FINANCIAL BLESSING

As you prepare your heart to give, consider the potential of each and every dollar that you hold in your hand. Then, give in faith that the full potential of your offering will be released into the world, to do His will on earth, and bring truth to those who are trapped by the lies and ignorance of the enemy.

WEEK 24
Giving with a Price Tag

Now Araunah said to David, "Let my lord the king take and offer up whatever seems good to him. Look, here are oxen for burnt sacrifice, and threshing implements and the yokes of the oxen for wood. All these, O king, Araunah has given to the king." And Araunah said to the king, "May the LORD your God accept you." Then the king said to Araunah, "No, but I will surely buy it from you for a price; nor will I offer burnt offerings to the LORD my God with that which costs me nothing." So David bought the threshing floor and the oxen for fifty shekels of silver. And David built there an altar to the LORD, and offered burnt offerings and peace offerings. So the LORD heeded the prayers for the land, and the plague was withdrawn from Israel.

—2 SAMUEL 24:22–25

KING DAVID COMMITTED a sin in the eyes of the Lord by having a census taken of Israel and Judah against His will. It was a sin because God's strength is not in numbers, and He does not want us to depend on it, either. He is our strength and victory. The Lord can do more with one faithful person than with a multitude who put their trust in the strength and ability of numbers. In today's world, numbers equal success and power, but God is looking for obedient hearts.

Only after the number of the soldiers in the nation was brought to David did he realize that he had sinned. Just at that time, the prophet Gad came in and announced to him the Lord's penalty for that sin, and seventy thousand people fell by the plague that day. The prophet's advice to him was to build an altar for a sacrifice unto the Lord on the threshing floor of Araunah, the Jebusite, to see if it would stop the plague.

Sacrificial giving still touches the heart of God today.

As a repentant David approached the threshing floor, Araunah offered his oxen, implements, and threshing floor to the king as a gift for his sacrifice. But David refused it, saying, "…nor will I offer burnt offerings to the Lord my God with that which costs me nothing." He bought everything from Arauna at the true price, offered his sacrifice, and the plague stopped.

Thank God, we do not have to bring offerings for our sins anymore, but our sacrificial giving still touches the heart of God today.

WEEK 25
Freewill Offerings

And when you offer a sacrifice of thanksgiving to the LORD, offer it of your own free will.

—LEVITICUS 22:29

GOD INSTRUCTED THE Israelites to bring all kinds of offerings at different times and occasions. There were offerings for sins and for different festivities and situations, most of which were embedded in the law. The people under the Old Covenant lived a lifestyle of continuous offerings that must have cost them much, but the law was the law and they had no other choice.

Freewill offerings come from joyful, grateful hearts.

On top of all the many offerings and sacrifices that they were obliged to bring, God also introduced the offering of thanksgiving, which was to be a freewill offering. He not only wanted to see their obedience to the law, but also their love for Him as they decided for themselves the value of their offering.

Thanksgiving cannot be legislated, it has to come from the heart and that is what He desires from us. He gave you a free will and wants to see how you use it—selfishly on yourself, or honoring Him with it.

The freewill offering was not limited to the Old Testament. Paul also refers to it in 2 Corinthians 9:7, "So let each one give as he purposes in his heart, not grudgingly or of necessity; for God loves a cheerful giver."

Freewill offerings come from joyful, grateful hearts. God does not appreciate manipulated giving, or, as Paul puts it, "grudgingly or of necessity," but happy givers. Since one tenth of our income is the Lord's, anyway, freewill offerings come on top of the tithe, which means offerings only begin after you have already given your full tithe.

Take some time to first count your blessings. Then, determine in your heart what you want to give as your thanksgiving offering.

SECRETS OF FINANCIAL BLESSING

The Better Sacrifice

By faith Abel offered God a better sacrifice than Cain did. By faith he was commended as a righteous man, when God spoke well of his offerings. And by faith he still speaks, even though he is dead.
—HEBREWS 11:4, NIV

Do not be like Cain, who belonged to the evil one and murdered his brother. And why did he murder him? Because his own actions were evil and his brother's were righteous.
—1 JOHN 3:12, NIV

NOT ALL SACRIFICES are the same before the Lord. He accepts some and rejects others. It is not that He needs our money; all the silver and gold belong to Him, anyway. *We* are the ones with needs; we need to give more than He needs to receive.

An offering given without faith can
do more harm than good.

Cain brought some offerings of his vegetables to the Lord while Abel brought an offering of his flock. Abel brought his offering "by faith," while Cain obviously did not, and that made all the difference in the eyes of the Lord.

God accepted Abel's offer, and, although his life was cut short, his testimony lives on to this day and earned him a place in the Bible's "Hall of Faith."

…And by faith he still speaks, even though he is dead.
—HEBREWS 11:4, NIV

God spoke well of Abel's offering because he gave it in faith. Cain's story tells us that an offering given without faith can do more harm than good. If you cannot give in faith and with the intention to honor the Lord, it is better not to give at all. God is not a beggar who needs alms to make a living. He is after our hearts! The condition of your heart means far more to Him than all the money you can give.

Give a better sacrifice by searching your heart, and be sure to give in faith and with joy. God *loves* a cheerful giver!

WEEK 27
Proper Protocol

For the LORD is great and greatly to be praised; He is to be feared above all gods. For all the gods of the peoples are idols, but the LORD made the heavens. Honor and majesty are before Him; strength and beauty are in His sanctuary. Give to the LORD, O families of the peoples, give to the LORD glory and strength. Give to the LORD the glory due His name; bring an offering, and come into His courts. Oh, worship the LORD in the beauty of holiness! Tremble before Him, all the earth.

—PSALM 96:4–9

As a minister, I am privileged to travel to different parts of the world regularly. Every time I travel, I take gifts with me for the people I will be visiting. Everybody always appreciates a gift that comes from another country, knowing that there are people who care about them. I always love it when they open the gifts right away to share the moment with them.

God is well able and willing to help
you in a time of need.

When it comes to "visiting" with the Lord as we draw close to Him in fellowship and prayer in the sanctuary, we do not always think of our offering in terms of creating a special moment with Him. We usually see Him as the One who gives because we are the needy ones, and our attitude is often to receive something from Him.

Proper protocol is in order when we draw near to God. He is high above all else and worthy to be honored with our best, "Honor and majesty are before Him." You do not rush into the King's presence unprepared and empty-handed!

David, a king himself, knew all about protocol, and in the psalm above he describes how to draw near to the Lord, "Give to the Lord glory and strength," and "Give to the Lord the glory due His name."

Recognize and acknowledge that He is God, that He is glorious and majestic, well able and willing to help you in a time of need. "Bring an offering, and come into His courts" (v. 8).

God is looking forward to sharing a special moment with you!

WEEK 28
God's Antidote for Greed

*For the love of money is a root of all kinds of evil, for which some
have strayed from the faith in their greediness, and pierced themselves through with many sorrows.*

—1 Timothy 6:10

Greed is one of the most dangerous forces known to us. It is
described as "an excessive desire to acquire or possess more than
what one needs, and an addiction to material wealth."[1] Greed makes
people ruthless and cruel in their selfish quest for wealth. Paul warns
Timothy that greed is able to lead believers astray and cause them
to "pierce *themselves* through with many sorrows," turning villains
into victims of their own wickedness. Greed becomes particularly
dangerous when the desire for more denies others their rights.

The best antidote for greed is giving
from a generous heart.

There is nothing wrong with the desire to prosper for the right
reasons. Money is neither the root nor reason of any evil. But the
lust for money is evil. Shallow believers are quick to defend the
popular belief that poverty is noble and wealth evil, all based on a
misunderstanding of this verse. Money only becomes evil when it
falls in to the hands of evil people, but it can do much good, also.
We sometimes hear people with religious schizophrenia complain
about their lack of money while, at the same time, they constantly
pray and preach against it.

The Bible puts greed on the same line with gross evils such as
stealing, drunkenness, revilers, and extortionists (1 Corinthians
6:10) and warns that such people will not inherit the kingdom of
God. Greed can keep you out of God's kingdom!

The best antidote for greed is giving from a generous heart. What
you give away cannot control you. Money has the potential to either

pierce you through with many sorrows, or bless you, depending on how you handle it. But, remember, it is more blessed to give than to receive.

WEEK 29
The Purpose of Wealth

And you shall remember the Lord your God, for it is He who gives you power to get wealth, that He may establish His covenant which He swore to your fathers, as it is this day.

—DEUTERONOMY 8:18

WEALTH, LIKE EVERYTHING else that God created, has a specific purpose. God created wealth, not poverty. He put Adam in an environment with everything he needed to live well. He gave him all the trees and herbs with their fruit, even good gold and precious stones. The Old Testament opens with wealth, and so does the New Testament. When Jesus announced His earthly ministry in Luke 4:18, the very first thing He mentioned was to bring good news to the poor. Even His first miracle was one of provision.

The purpose of wealth is to establish
God's covenant on the earth.

The Israelites knew what poverty was when they lived in Egypt as slaves. After 430 years of oppression, there was nothing left of the riches of Abraham, but when they left, they had great wealth. God worked out a plan to put treasures in their hands. He had a purpose for that wealth, and that was to build a tabernacle where His presence could dwell.

In the verse above, God reminds the people of Israel that He is the One who gives them the power to get wealth, and that the purpose of that wealth is to establish His covenant on the earth. God's covenant with Abram was a covenant of enormous blessing, "I will bless you...you shall be a blessing" (Gen. 12:2). It is hard to get a poor person, who struggles to make ends meet, to believe that God is good unless you can convince them that He wants them, too, to be blessed.

A prosperous life is defined by having enough to provide well for your own family, while also having enough to help the poor and support the work of the gospel.

Your money has a purpose that goes beyond your own personal needs. Giving is working with God to establish His covenant of blessing on the earth.

WEEK 30
Growing Your Account

Not that I seek the gift, but I seek the fruit that abounds to your account.
—PHILIPPIANS 4:17

Not that I'm looking for handouts, but I do want you to experience the blessing that issues from generosity.
—PHILIPPIANS 4:17, THE MESSAGE

W E KNOW THAT our ways are not God's ways (Isaiah 55:8–9) because His ways are higher than ours. God does not think the way we do because His logic is not the same as ours, but He wants us to come up to His ways so that we can live above the standards of our fallen world. This is also true when it comes to finances.

Blessings flow from a partnership with the Lord.

Some people are fearful, even angry, when it comes to giving. We once had a visitor in our church who loved all about the service. She loved the praise and worship and seemed to enjoy the atmosphere of celebration, but when we prepared to bring our tithes and offerings, she got up and left. She apparently thought the church was only there only to take from other people.

When offering time comes, we should rejoice and be glad for it offers us an opportunity to grow our account, not only our heavenly account, but also the one on earth. Paul taught the believers of Philippi that giving to the work of the ministry is not a handout that they give, but an opportunity to "experience the blessing that issues from generosity" (v. 17, THE MESSAGE). This is how you should see offering time at your church. Blessings flow from a partnership with the Lord.

God gives to givers so that they can continue to give. That's how His economy works, and by your giving you participate in it.

WEEK 31
God Will Supply...in All of Your Needs?

And my God shall supply all your need according to His riches in glory by Christ Jesus.

—PHILIPPIANS 4:19

SOME CHRISTIANS "CONFESS" this verse, thinking that just by speaking it, all their financial needs will be met. It is true, of course, that God takes care of His children, if they allow Him to, but the promise in this verse has a condition to it.

When you finance the work of the Lord,
you bless to the Lord Himself.

The rich supply Paul talks about here is not a free-for-all; it applies only to those who sow into the work of the ministry. Paul wrote those words as a thank you note after the Philippian Christians sent him some support for his mission trips and his personal needs. Even if a minister has more than enough to do the work of his ministry, he will fail if he cannot support himself and his family. Ministers who do not receive an adequate income from their ministries are vulnerable in this area.

Paul calls the things they sent to him a "sweet-smelling aroma, an acceptable sacrifice, well-pleasing to God" (v. 18). While these people gave to Paul personally, their giving was a "sweet-smelling aroma, an acceptable sacrifice, well-pleasing to God" (Phil. 4:18). When you finance the work of the Lord, you bless to the Lord Himself.

As you plan your gift, be sure to present it as a sweet-smelling aroma to the Lord Himself, and expect in faith to receive the generosity that flows from the glory of the Lord to exceed yours. He wants to "supply all your needs according to His riches in glory by Christ Jesus" as His thank you note to you.

You can be sure that God will take care of everything you need, his generosity exceeding even yours in the glory that pours from Jesus.

—Philippians 4:19, The Message

When Taking Care of a
Need Is up to You

But Jesus said to them, "They do not need to go away. You give them something to eat."

—Matthew 14:16

How often do we find ourselves with little or nothing to give? Sometimes the need seems so much bigger than our resources. That is what happened to the disciples when they faced a hungry crowd of five thousand men, besides the women and children. They felt the best way to deal with the situation was to send the crowd away.

The only problem they had was that the Lord never sent anybody away, no matter what the need was. We cannot solve all the problems around us, but we should not be too quick to give up, either. He has ways and channels and resources that we do not know about.

When obedience and faith meet, we can
do that which He calls us to do.

It probably scared the disciples when the Lord told them, "*You* give them something to eat." They thought they were off the hook because they did not have what the people needed, but there was no way out of it. The fact that they could not help did not change His mind. His disciples got the assignment anyway.

"Bring them here to Me," He said (v. 18), and with that they handed Him the five loaves and two fish that they had with them.

The disciples almost argued themselves out of the most amazing experience. The little that they had was enough to set a miracle in motion right in front of their eyes. To the disciples, it looked as if the Lord was going to take their food and give all of it away, but they ended up with a basketful for each one of them.

When obedience and faith meet, we can do that which He calls us to do. The little you have can do more than you think.

Looking Beyond

Then Jesus, looking at him, loved him, and said to him, "One thing you lack: Go your way, sell whatever you have and give to the poor, and you will have treasure in heaven; and come, take up the cross, and follow Me."

—MARK 10:21

THE YOUNG MAN in this story was rich, yet there was still something missing in his life. He realised that there was at least one more thing he needed to have, and that was certainty about his eternal life. His earthly life was perfect, but he wanted to take care of his future. He had kept all the commandments from his youth and believed that he would get a good answer from the Lord, and he did. But still, he was not satisfied. Jesus knew exactly what it was, but did not tell him at first. He wanted to see if he was ready for the complete answer to his question.

Giving away his possessions did not
mean a life of poverty at all.

To surrender your life to the Lord is easier said than done. When you hear that you have to depend on Him for everything you will ever need, it is hard for someone who is used to having it all to accept. To trade a life of luxury for a cross is almost unthinkable.

The cross that Jesus had in mind was not the gold or silver jewelry that we wear around the neck these days, it was a horrible instrument of torture leading to certain death. With that, he was invited to join His band of disciples, an honor that would eternalize his name. But, it was too much for him and he walked away. All we know about him now is that He rejected the most generous offer that ever came his way. We do not know how well he lived or how much he owned; we do not even know his name!

What this young man did not know was that giving away his

possessions did not mean a life of poverty at all. The cross, tragic and sad as it would have seemed, had hidden in itself a treasure far beyond his earthly possessions. A life given is a life gained.

He who loves his life will lose it, and he who hates his life in this world will keep it for eternal life. (See John 12:25.)

WEEK 34
Eternal Treasures

Do not fear, little flock, for it is your Father's good pleasure to give you the kingdom. Sell what you have and give alms; provide yourselves money bags which do not grow old, a treasure in the heavens that does not fail, where no thief approaches nor moth destroys. For where your treasure is, there your heart will be also.

—LUKE 12:32–34

ONE OF THE mistakes we often make is to fit God into our norms, forgetting that His ways are higher than ours. In our thoughts, enough is equal to the need, but not according to the Lord. He is the God of more than enough. Jesus fed the crowds with more than they could eat. (See Matthew 14:15–21.) When the disciples went fishing at His command (Luke 5:6–7), they caught so many fish that their boats began to sink. After the devil stripped Job bare, God restored to him twice as much as he had before (Job 42:10), beside other blessings. Jesus says in John 10:10 that He came to give us life and that more abundantly.

When God rules as king in your heart, you will
never have to fear any lack of any good thing.

In the verses above, Jesus tells us, His disciples, not to worry about our daily needs because our Father, who cares for the lilies and the birds, will also care for us. Then He says that it is the Father's good pleasure to give us the kingdom. Who cares about giving away what you have if you can have the kingdom, knowing that where God rules there can be no shortage of any good thing.

As you consider your giving, do not think in terms of losing anything, but rather that you are a child of God and a citizen of His kingdom. Then, give with pleasure, just as it is God's pleasure to give you the kingdom. When God rules as king in your heart, you will never have to fear any lack of any good thing.

Be a person of faith and cross over into the kingdom of God!

WEEK 35
Confessing the Gospel of Christ

...while, through the proof of this ministry, they glorify God for the obedience of your confession to the gospel of Christ, and for your liberal sharing with them and all men...

—2 CORINTHIANS 9:13

WE ALL KNOW how important it is for believers to confess their faith in the Lord and His Word. The gospel is good news and we should be actively involved in making it known as far as we can. But spreading the gospel is not only done through preaching. The world has become immune to the gospel message because it has not always been delivered as good news. Far too many people have bad memories of their encounters with judgmental Christians. (It is much easier to condemn people than build them up.)

The very core of the gospel is a message of giving.

The simple basis of the gospel is that you cannot preach good news and be bad news. People ought to be glad when they see us coming. When we live the good news ourselves, more people will be willing to listen to what we have to say, especially when times are hard and they see us doing well with the blessing of the Lord upon our lives.

In the verse above, Paul says that the Judean saints, for which he received this offering, will "glorify God for the obedience of your confession to the gospel of Christ." These people confessed the good news by being the good news through their giving. The very core of the gospel is a message of giving: God gave His Son, Jesus gave His life, and then gave us new, abundant life and hope. Now, we give to make His goodness known to all men.

Talk is cheap, especially these days, but giving adds value to our confession of the gospel. In a world steeped in greed and selfishness, giving is rare and sure to attract attention. As your church flourishes through your giving, especially in tough times, the true value of the gospel will be made known to those outside. Giving is not just giving money away. It is confessing to the gospel of Jesus Christ.

WEEK 36
Stretching Your Money

ONE OF THE amazing things about inviting the Lord into your finances is how He can make it go further than it can in the natural. When His work becomes your work, you will find that you are able to do much more with the money you have, whether little or much. During the nine years that we were missionaries in Europe, we actually became used to it. To this day, we do not always know how we could do what we did with the money we had. Sometimes, money came from people or at times when we did not expected anything, but at other times we were just able to meet our family's needs with very little.

God knows how to stretch our money to
go all the way until every need is met.

The Bible has some of those stories, too. In 1 Kings 17, God sent Elijah to a widow in Zarephath to take care of him during a time of famine. She was busy preparing a dinner for her and her son with the very last flour and oil that she had. The prophet demanded to eat first of that food, before she and her son would eat of it. In the natural, this seems to be a cruel, selfish thing to do, but looking at it spiritually, the prophet activated a principle that would help this widow and her son through a time of scarcity in the land. We know that everything has two pictures, a natural and a spiritual, and we need to see both before we draw conclusions. The end of that story is that the oil in the jar and the flour in the bin did not run out until the drought was over.

In the New Testament, Jesus once fed five thousand hungry men, not counting the women and children, with five loaves and two fish—the meal of a boy. On another occasion, He fed four thousand people with seven loaves and a few fish.

In all three of these events, the little that was available became much and met the needs that were present. God can do it. But in all of the cases, the little that these people had, had to be given before it became much. When believers hold on to what they have, they may find out that it is all that they will have to work with. We have all heard the old saw, "At the end of my money, I still have a lot of month left." God knows how to stretch our money to go all the way until every need is met.

When your budget is small, be sure to include giving to the Lord as part of it and trust Him to take care of your needs.

WEEK 37
Increasing the Fruit of
Your Righteousness

Now may He who supplies seed to the sower, and bread for food, supply and multiply the seed you have sown and increase the fruits of your righteousness.

—2 Corinthians 9:10

For we are His workmanship, created in Christ Jesus for good works, which God prepared beforehand that we should walk in them.

—Ephesians 2:10

And let our people also learn to maintain good works, to meet urgent needs, that they may not be unfruitful.

—Titus 3:14

Jesus says in John 15:8 that the Father is glorified when we bear much fruit. He says that this is how we become His disciples and how we please the Father. He even says that we will be pruned to bear more fruit.

The "fruit of righteousness" is the fruit that we bear as the result of Christ living in us. His life in us enables us to do more than we can in our own strength. It is through our giving that the life of Christ is truly manifested in and through us. Good works can only come through giving, whether it is money, time, talents, or anything else.

Righteousness is right standing with God, with nothing separating you from Him. It is a gift that was purchased for you by the blood of Jesus when He died on the cross. It is a blessing of God's grace. It is a gift that keeps on giving as the fruit of our righteousness is increased when we give. This is our normal life in Christ and the very culture of God's kingdom.

Good works can only come through giving, whether it is money, time, talents, or anything else.

Nobody wants to stand before the Lord with empty hands on that great day. If you are a giver, God will give you seed to sow, and then multiply it as you do, and on top of that, increase the fruit of your righteousness.

WEEK 38
Lovers of Money

"No servant can serve two masters; for either he will hate the one and love the other, or else he will be loyal to the one and despise the other. You cannot serve God and mammon." Now the Pharisees, who were lovers of money, also heard all these things, and they derided Him.

—LUKE 16:13–14

JESUS WAS HAVING an interesting day with the Pharisees. He had just told a parable to teach a lesson on stewardship, but it offended them. As religious as they were, they were lovers of money, and lovers of money love to *have* money, but not to *give* money.

Although we do not have the title of *pharisee* in our churches anymore, that same spirit is alive and well today. Pharisees are willing to do all kinds of religious things, but they become hostile when they hear about giving money, especially in the church. Religious people serve mammon with their hearts and the Lord with their lips. They believe that the church should always give, but they do not care how the church is supposed to get what it is supposed to give.

Stewards of the Lord give hope to the hopeless.

The Pharisees derided the Lord; they ridiculed and expressed contempt for Him, and this attitude is well known today. Modern lovers of money have good excuses and witty one-liners, always ready to defend themselves. They are the kind that gives the gospel of glory a bad name, and neither saint nor sinner has any time for them.

Lovers of money find themselves in the bad company of the Pharisees, but stewards of the Lord give hope to the hopeless.

You either serve mammon or mammon serves you, and any compromise comes from the spirit of the Pharisees.

Deep down in your heart, you have only one Master.

WEEK 39
Two Kinds of Riches

He who is faithful in what is least is faithful also in much; and he who is unjust in what is least is unjust also in much. Therefore if you have not been faithful in the unrighteous mammon, who will commit to your trust the true riches?

—LUKE 16:10–11

H E WHO IS faithful in what is least is faithful also in much," because faithfulness is an attitude that has nothing to with amounts of money. The same goes for unfaithfulness. A tithe is a tithe, no matter the amount; the size of it is a token of God's blessing on one's life.

This is a story about stewardship, which is the story of every life. We came into this world with nothing. Everything we have was entrusted to us in a stewardship arrangement. It is God's provision of gifts, health, and opportunities that brings wealth into our lives.

A giving attitude will protect you against
the destructive power of greed.

Although mammon is material wealth, faithfulness to God is required. Jesus said that material wealth is not true riches, which means there are two kinds of riches and we will do well to discern accurately between them. The Lord also said that the true riches will not be committed to the trust of those who are unfaithful in the unrighteous mammon.

Faithfulness in the unrighteous mammon means honesty at work with good quality service, honesty in business, and, of course, giving to the Lord what belongs to Him.

You are either a steward or an owner. It is when we see what is entrusted to us as possessions that mammon tightens its grip on our lives. The devil does not care whether you are rich or poor, healthy or sick. He will give you anything as long as it can separate you from God. He robs you of the true riches by giving you an appetite for the false. A giving attitude will protect you against the destructive power of greed and increase your true riches.

WEEK 40
An Audience with the King

Give to the LORD the glory due His name; Bring an offering, and come into His courts. Oh, worship the LORD in the beauty of holiness! Tremble before Him, all the earth.

—PSALM 96:8–9

JUST IMAGINE THE splendour and glory of the Lord's courts! We have glimpses of what the throne room looks like in Isaiah 6 and some passages in Revelation, and it is an awesome sight. Even the angels and other heavenly beings that live in His presence continually stand in awe of His beauty.

Isaiah heard the seraphim say to one another, "Holy, holy, holy is the Lord of hosts; the whole earth is full of His glory!" They spoke with such conviction and awe that the doorposts were trembling at the sound of their voices.

We can join in the praises of heaven even now.

When the apostle John saw the Lord in a vision on the island of Patmos (Revelation 1:9–17), he fell at His feet as though dead, and *that* after he walked with Him for more than three years on the earth. In this vision, however, he saw the resurrected Lord in His glory.

The psalm above proclaims the greatness of the Lord and calls on us to give to Him the glory due His name (v. 8). Consider that our earthly voices blend with the perfect voices of those holy beings before the throne! Although not perfect, our voices are very special to God because we were once lost, but we now are saved.

While on the earth, we can enter His courts by faith and experience His presence while in the flesh because Jesus took our sins away. We can join in the praises of heaven even now.

Who would think of an offering in such glorious moments? According to David, it is quite in order, "Bring an offering and come into His courts." Draw near to Him in the beauty of holiness with an offering to the King in your hand!

JOHAN DU TOIT

63

WEEK 41
A Memorial Before God

There was a certain man in Caesarea called Cornelius, a centurion of what was called the Italian Regiment, a devout man and one who feared God with all his household, who gave alms generously to the people, and prayed to God always. About the ninth hour of the day he saw clearly in a vision an angel of God coming in and saying to him, "Cornelius!" And when he observed him, he was afraid, and said, "What is it, lord?" So he said to him, "Your prayers and your alms have come up for a memorial before God."

—ACTS 10:1–4

A MEMORIAL IS A monument to honor a special person or event. Impressive monuments have been built through the centuries to remind generations of the accomplishments of great people. Monuments have inspiring stories to tell that should never be forgotten.

Your prayers and alms are building
your memorial before the Lord.

Cornelius was a Roman soldier, the leader of a regiment of the occupying force in Israel. Needless to say, the Romans were not popular with the Jews. They had no respect for gentiles to begin with, least of all for those who ruled over them. In addition, it was forbidden for Jews to even go into a gentile's house. (See Acts 10:38.)

Cornelius was a gentile, but he believed in God and prayed to Him. He also "gave alms generously to the people." As he was praying one day, an angel appeared to him, telling him, "Your prayers and alms have come up as a memorial before God." He did not know it, but he had a monument before God. That means that God could not forget him; his name was always before Him.

Who would not like to have a memorial before God? That must be the greatest honor anyone can ever wish for. Your prayers and alms are building your memorial before the Lord. He cannot forget you, He knows your name, and He will look for special ways to bless you just as He did for Cornelius.

WEEK 42
Rejected Offerings

So let each one give as he purposes in his heart, not grudgingly or of necessity; for God loves a cheerful giver.

—2 CORINTHIANS 9:7

OD DOES NOT always accept our gifts. He refused Cain's offering in Genesis 4:5, and He told the Israelites that He had no delight in theirs in Isaiah 1:11–14 because their hearts were far from Him. They legalistically gave the prescribed offerings, but their hearts were far from God. They gave for their own selfish reasons because God was obligated to bless them according to the Law, but it was nothing but lip service. God actually told them to keep their offerings, that He hated their assemblies, and said that their incense was an abomination to Him.

These were harsh words, but God cannot be bribed and His favor is not for sale. He does not need our money; when we give, *we* are the ones who are blessed by it.

If you cannot give with joy, it is better not to give at all.

Those Israelites thought they could manipulate God by their offerings, forcing Him to bless them with rain and good crops. What they did not understand was that the Lord wanted their love and desired their fellowship more than their offerings. But their hearts were calloused and things went horribly wrong for them. God even said that He would not listen to their prayers (Isaiah 1:15), that their weeping and crying did not impress Him, and that He would not accept their offerings in goodwill anymore (Malachi 2:13).

The joy in your heart is what He is looking for. Your church may accept your offering, but it is your joy that makes it acceptable to the Lord. Do not just give out of necessity because there is a need. Give because you have decided to in your heart. If you cannot give with joy, it is better not to give at all.

SECRETS OF FINANCIAL BLESSING

WEEK 43
Honesty in Giving

Ananias and Sapphira died in church after they lied about their offerings. They sold a piece of land and brought some of the proceeds and "laid it at the apostle's feet" (Acts 5:2). That was a wonderful thing to do, except that they lied and said that it was *all* the proceeds of the sale, not just part of it.

Nobody asked them to give all of that money to the church; neither was there a law that required them to do so. For some reason, it was a popular thing to do in those days (Acts 4:34–37), but still it was their prerogative to decide how much they wanted to give. The problem was not the amount, but that they lied about it.

When you bring your tithe, be honest with God.

That lie cost them their lives. The church was pure in those days and it was dangerous to bring any sin into it, as these two found out. If only they were honest about it, they could have lived full lives and received a wonderful reward from the Lord on top of it.

Once again, the condition of your heart matters to God. Ananias and Sapphira thought they were just lying to the church, but, in fact, they were lying to the Holy Spirit:

> While it remained, was it not your own? And after it was sold, was it not in your own control? Why have you conceived this thing in your heart? You have not lied to men but to God.
>
> —Acts 5:4

Today, this incident seems like harsh punishment for a small sin. Yet, God saw it differently.

When you bring your tithe, be honest with God. Let it be a full tithe, not just a part of it. If it is not a tithe, do not call it a tithe. Let's keep the church pure by being honest before God in all things.

WEEK 44
Givers and Takers

SOMEBODY ONCE SAID that, when a baby is born, its hands are clenched in a fist, but when a person becomes born again, his hands open up. This seems to be the case when it comes to giving, anyway. When all that you have is what you can see with your eyes, it makes no sense to give any of it away. If Christ is not your hope, your tangible possessions will mean everything to you. The more you have of them, the better life you may look forward to.

One meeting with the Lord turned a taker into a giver.

Zacchaeus was fortunate to work for the tax office, and with that came the opportunity to line his pockets with taxpayer's money. His love for money drove him to take from people who came to him to pay their taxes.

Then, a day came when Zacchaeus met the Lord Jesus. He was a short person and had to climb up a tree to be able to see Him as He passed by. Jesus looked up the tree, called him down, and told him that He was going to stay at his house for the day. That meeting changed Zacchaeus's life and cured his lust for money:

> Then Zacchaeus stood and said to the Lord, "Look, Lord, I give half of my goods to the poor; and if I have taken anything from anyone by false accusation, I restore fourfold."
> —LUKE 19:8

Zacchaeus's entire life was turned around in a single day. Suddenly, his hands opened up to give back four times more than he took. On top of that, he pledged half of what he owned to the poor. One meeting with the Lord turned a taker into a giver. And, as far as we know, Jesus never even spoke with him about money.

Money lost its attraction when Zacchaeus met the Lord. He found the One who enriched his life beyond anything money can buy. Have you found the true riches yet?

WEEK 45
The Lord Will Provide

A BRAHAM EARNED A very special place in the heart of God, and in the Bible's "Hall of Faith." (See Hebrews 11.) The "father of all who believe" (Rom. 4:11) passed test after test in his walk with God. The most gruelling of tests came when God told him to sacrifice Isaac as a burnt offering on Mount Moriah. (See Genesis 22:1–2.) Without debating the matter with the Lord, Abraham left to do as the Lord commanded him. His faith in God was so strong that he believed fully that the Lord would raise his son from the dead. (See Hebrews 11:19.)

> If you know Him as "The Lord Will Provide," you
> can freely give as He inspires you to do.

Just when Abraham stretched out his hand to slay Isaac with the knife, the angel of the Lord stopped him and showed him a ram that was caught in the thicket by its horns, and he offered it instead.

Abraham was willing to give his only, beloved son, the one he received by a promise from God. We now know what Abraham did not know back then, namely that God would also be willing to give His only Son to save the world from the bondage of sin.

> And He said, "Do not lay your hand on the lad, or do anything to him; for now I know that you fear God, since you have not withheld your son, your only son, from Me."
> —GENESIS 22:12

As Abraham passed this test of giving to the Lord the most precious gift that he ever had, God revealed Himself to him in a fresh, new way with a new name: *Jehovah Jireh*, "The Lord Will Provide." From that day on he knew the Lord as his Provider.

He is still *Jehovah Jireh* today. If you know Him as "The Lord

Will Provide," you can freely give as He inspires you to do, without any fear that you will ever run out of anything.

That step of faith on Abraham's part brought a fresh new revelation of God to Him.

God Gives...and Take Away?

And he said: "Naked I came from my mother's womb, And naked shall I return there. The Lord gave, and the Lord has taken away; blessed be the name of the Lord."

—JOB 1:21

THIS IS ONE of the best-known verses in the Bible, especially by people who have a twisted image of God. Who wants to trust God if He takes away everything dear to you?

It was not God who took away from Job, but the devil.

Well, there is quite a bit more to this story. When Job spoke these words, he did not know what he was talking about. It is wise to finish a book before you make up your mind!

This one verse became the foundation of a faulty doctrine. It is quoted at funerals everywhere every day. It inspires songs that are sung in many churches and it forms a skewed perception of the character of God in the minds of countless saints and sinners around the world. Of course, it was not God who took away from Job, but the devil. Satan is the thief and destroyer and murderer, according to John 10:10.

All through this difficult time, there was no lack of doomsayers in Job's life. But he refused to be swayed by any of them. He knew that God was out there somewhere, and that He would come to his aid and deliver him. He could not make any sense of what was going on in his life, but he did understand the character of God and continued to put his trust in Him.

At the end of it all, Job was much wiser and more blessed than he was in the beginning and he revealed God's true character to us.

I know that You can do everything, and that no purpose of Yours can be withheld from You. You asked, "Who is this who hides counsel without knowledge?" Therefore I have uttered what I did not understand, things too wonderful for me, which I did not know.

—Job 42:2–3

Secrets of Financial Blessing

WEEK 47
To Honor a King

Now after Jesus was born in Bethlehem of Judea in the days of Herod the king, behold, wise men from the East came to Jerusalem....When they saw the star, they rejoiced with exceedingly great joy. And when they had come into the house, they saw the young Child with Mary His mother, and fell down and worshiped Him. And when they had opened their treasures, they presented gifts to Him: gold, frankincense, and myrrh.

—MATTHEW 2:1, 10–11

SOME SCHOLARS BELIEVE that the wise men who brought these gifts to the infant Jesus were non-Jewish religious astrologers who found out about the birth of a great Jewish king when they saw a special star in the sky. They decided that the appropriate thing to do was to go to there and honor Him with gifts fit for a king.

You never go to a meeting with a king empty-handed. Even when queen Sheba, a royal herself, went to meet King Solomon, she took gifts with her:

You never go to a meeting with a king empty-handed.

Now when the queen of Sheba heard of the fame of Solomon, she came to Jerusalem to test Solomon with hard questions, having a very great retinue, camels that bore spices, gold in abundance, and precious stones; and when she came to Solomon, she spoke with him about all that was in her heart.

—2 CHRONICLES 9:1–12

The gifts of these wise men started a tradition that is followed around the world to this day. As you think of the gifts that you will give at Christmas, make sure the Lord is at the top of your list. And do not be tempted to use your tithe to buy gifts for others. Honor Him as King of kings and Lord of your life first of all.

JOHAN DU TOIT   73

WEEK 48
The Focus on Him

Then Mary took a pound of very costly oil of spikenard, anointed the feet of Jesus, and wiped His feet with her hair. And the house was filled with the fragrance of the oil.

—JOHN 12:3

VERY EXPENSIVE GIFTS were given to Jesus at the beginning and end of His life on earth. The wise men brought gifts of gold, frankincense, and myrrh at His birth. Shortly before His death on the cross, Mary brought some very expensive oil of spikenard and anointed His feet with it. Spikenard is a flowering plant that grows in the Himalayas of China, India, and Nepal. The spikenard stems and roots are crushed and distilled into a thick, intensely aromatic essential oil used as a perfume, an incense, a sedative, and an herbal medicine said to fight insomnia, birth difficulties, and other minor ailments. No doubt, it is something very special.

Mary's worship cost her dearly, but
it was not wealth lost.

Immediately after she poured that oil out on Him, some started to criticize her. Judas commented, "Why was this fragrant oil not sold for three hundred denarii and given to the poor?" (John 12:5). The value of that ointment was equal to a year's wages for a worker; a handy amount of money. But it was not the poor that Judas was concerned about. "This he said, not that he cared for the poor, but because he was a thief, and had the money box; and he used to take what was put in it" (v. 6).

Mary's worship cost her dearly, but it was not wealth lost. Her adoration of the Lord filled the whole house with a lovely fragrance and everybody shared in that blessing. When she left that house, she had the same fragrance on her that Jesus had on Him, a glorious worship experience to her and Him.

Giving to the Lord revealed her heart as well as Judas's. While the money she spent on Him is long gone, the story of her worship lives on.

WEEK 49
True Riches

There was a certain rich man who had a steward, and an accusation was brought to him that this man was wasting his goods. So he called him and said to him, "What is this I hear about you? Give an account of your stewardship, for you can no longer be steward." Then the steward said within himself, "What shall I do? For my master is taking the stewardship away from me. I cannot dig; I am ashamed to beg. I have resolved what to do, that when I am put out of the stewardship, they may receive me into their houses." So he called every one of his master's debtors to him, and said to the first, "How much do you owe my master?" And he said, "A hundred measures of oil." So he said to him, "Take your bill, and sit down quickly and write fifty." Then he said to another, "And how much do you owe?" So he said, "A hundred measures of wheat." And he said to him, "Take your bill, and write eighty." So the master commended the unjust steward because he had dealt shrewdly....He who is faithful in what is least is faithful also in much; and he who is unjust in what is least is unjust also in much. Therefore if you have not been faithful in the unrighteous mammon, who will commit to your trust the true riches? And if you have not been faithful in what is another man's, who will give you what is your own?

—LUKE 16:1–8, 10–12

T HE MANAGER FROM this parable got into trouble because it was discovered that he looked out more for his own interests than doing the job he was paid for. He clearly abused his privileged position. When he got caught and realised that his lavish lifestyle was about to come to an end, he figured out a way to take care of himself. He quickly went to all his boss's debtors and did them the favor of reducing their debt, hoping that they would return the favor by taking him into their homes when he became homeless. He first worked for money; now, money was working for him. Twisted as this plan was, his boss complimented him on it for his shrewdness.

Be smart. Do not work for mammon—
let mammon work for you.

Because he knew how to look after himself. Streetwise people are smarter in this regard than law-abiding citizens. They are on constant alert, looking for angles, surviving by their wits. I want you to be smart in the same way—but for what is right—using every adversity to stimulate you to creative survival, to concentrate your attention on the bare essentials, so you'll live, really live, and not complacently just get by on good behavior.

—LUKE 16:8–9, THE MESSAGE

This man's troubles began when he tried to serve two masters at the same time: his indulgent lifestyle and his boss. But, deep down, he was loyal only to himself. Unfaithfulness works in much just as it does in scarcity. There are only two kinds of riches: temporary earthly luxuries that fade away, and the rich rewards of a faithful life lived to please the Lord.

Be smart. Do not work for mammon—let mammon work for you.

WEEK 50
Increasing While Scattering

There is one who scatters, yet increases more; and there is one who withholds more than is right, but it leads to poverty. The generous soul will be made rich, and he who waters will also be watered himself.
—PROVERBS 11:24–25

GOD'S RECIPE NEVER changes from the beginning to the end—if you want to receive, you must first give. This goes squarely against the grain of the carnal mind, which is why so many fight this basic principle. The Word was given to us as the thoughts of God. (See Isaiah 55:8–11.) The just shall live by faith, according to Romans 1:17, and for those who are willing to step into a life of faith, wonderful new adventures of God's provision are waiting.

If you cannot give in faith, it is better not to give at all.

I often hear from believers that it is necessary to separate Scripture from reality. I have always believed that Scripture is God's reality and that He wants to make it our reality as a testimony of His goodness. His ways are higher than our ways so that we may walk higher than we can in our own strength. If that is not possible, everything else in the Bible is just a fable. You either believe the reality of the world system, or you believe the reality of the Word.

A Christian leader once asked for my opinion on a situation in which he found himself. He was trapped in a situation of financial lack and wanted to know if it would be fine to be excused from tithing until he solved his problems. I had deep sympathy for him, but I was not going to offer advice that is contrary to the Word. He was looking for what he thought was a sensible solution, but it would have made his faith redundant. It would place man's wisdom on a higher level than God's.

Here is God's wisdom, as I understand it: you give yourself out of trouble, but if you cannot give in faith, it is better not to give at all.

WEEK 51
Testing God

"Bring all the tithes into the storehouse, that there may be food in My house, and try Me now in this," Says the Lord of hosts, "If I will not open for you the windows of heaven and pour out for you such blessing that there will not be room enough to receive it."

—MALACHI 3:10

A S FAR AS I know, money is the only matter where God invites man to test Him. He put His own integrity on the line here in this passage from Malachi, which tells us that our giving is important to Him. It also shows that He wants to pour out abundant blessing upon us.

There are two ways to try test the Lord when the issue is money: to prove that He does what He says He will do, and to prove that He does not do what He promises to. In my years of ministry I have seen both. Some people have told me that tithing does not work. They gave their tithe, but they ended up worse off than they were before their tithing. They felt that they had proved to themselves that tithing does not work; that it was all empty religious talk and fundraising for the church. But there have been others who told me their testimonies of how their financial situations turned around when they started tithing. They proved the Lord in this and found Him to be true to His promises.

You may test the Lord in your finances, but
your faith has already shaped the outcome.

The Israelites tested the Lord as they walked in circles through the wilderness and were dying in the desert. (See Hebrews 3:9.) Ten of the spies that Moses sent out to Canaan believed they were unable to take possession of the Promised Land, and, in the end, they were right. Two of them believed that they were well able to possess the land, and they were also right.

What this shows is, you can get what you believe—if you believe that honoring the Lord with your tithes and offerings will release His blessing to you, it can happen, while on the other hand, if you believe that it will not work for you, it won't.

You may test the Lord in your finances, but your faith has already shaped the outcome.

WEEK 52
The Rewards from Men and the Rewards from God

Take heed that you do not do your charitable deeds before men, to be seen by them. Otherwise you have no reward from your Father in heaven. Therefore, when you do a charitable deed, do not sound a trumpet before you as the hypocrites do in the synagogues and in the streets, that they may have glory from men. Assuredly, I say to you, they have their reward. But when you do a charitable deed, do not let your left hand know what your right hand is doing, that your charitable deed may be in secret; and your Father who sees in secret will Himself reward you openly. —MATTHEW 6:1–4

EVERYTHING HAS TWO pictures, namely visible and invisible; a natural and a spiritual. There is the part that everybody can see, and then there is the part that only God sees, which can be things that people do that inspires others, but it also touches the heart of God in some way. This is what Jesus talks about in the above passage.

You either work for man's accolades, or God's reward.

When you do something praiseworthy, He says, do not use it to impress others who might applaud you, because that will be the only reward you will get. Some people are addicted to the approval of others. They will do anything for it. When they give, they help themselves more than the ones they are helping. The admiration of man is a poor reward compared to what God can do.

Faith plays a very subtle role here. You either work for man's accolades, or God's reward.

When you do a charitable deed, keep it to yourself as well as you can. Do it as unto the Lord. Do not advertise it with the idea of scoring points with anybody. Your Father who sees in secret will reward you openly, and it will be much more than any man can ever do for you.

Afterword

SMALL CHURCHES CAN do great things, much greater than they can through human efforts, when ordinary people embrace the principles of the Word and apply them in faith to their lives. God never depended on large crowds to accomplish His goals. He always looked for faithful people. It is sad to see churches compromise the standards of the Word to swell their numbers, which can, at best, give them an *outward appearance* of success. Large crowds never impressed God, but faithfulness always touches His heart. *Success is to do the will of God.* All we need to do to make it happen is to teach the simple principles of the Word. The Word produces fruit when its seed falls into the fertile soil of faithful hearts because it never returns to Him void.

Money follows vision. Every believer wants to be part of a vision that brings fulfillment to their lives and glory to the Lord. The vision of the church is given to us in the Word, not in fancy mission statements adopted from the corporations of the world. When we follow the Lord's simple instructions for the church, we will have what it takes to fulfill our call. We found it to work the same in affluent Canada as in war-ravaged Sudan. A blessed church begins with blessed members, and blessed members begin with sound teaching.

Our task to take the gospel to all nations is huge and we cannot do it without God's blessing. We certainly cannot do it in our own strength or with our own budget. The cost of travel, accommodation, and resources is astronomical, but we can do it if every believer becomes a giver. We can win our battles and overcome our obstacles when every believer contributes to the cause. And it begins with having God's heart and understanding His thoughts so that we may walk the high road to His glory.

Notes

PREFACE

1. *Merriam-Webster's Collegiate Dictionary, 11th Edition* (Springfield, MA: Merriam-Webster, 2003).

WEEK 16

1. A. S. Crockett, "George C. Boldt's Life a Continuous Romance: Reminiscences of Waldorf-Astoria Proprietor, Who Rose from the Kitchen to be the Most Famous Hotel Man in the World" (author's paraphrase), *The New York Times*, December 10, 1916, from Web site: http://query.nytimes.com/mem/archivefree/pdf?_r=1&res=9C0CE2D7153 BE233A25753C1A9649D946796D6CF (accessed February 16, 2010).

WEEK 28

1. *Merriam-Webster's Collegiate Dictionary, 11th Edition*, 2003.

About the Author

Pastor Johan du Toit was born and raised in a family of ministers in South Africa. After a season in the banking industry, he entered the ministry as a missionary pastor in Flanders, Belgium, with his wife and their two sons. They immigrated to Canada in 1999 and became Canadian citizens soon after. Together with his wife, Gerda, they pastor a church in Newmarket, Ontario. As the founder and president of WordWise Word School, Inc., an international correspondence Bible School, he also travels regularly to minister.

To Contact the Author

johanh.dutoit@gmail.com

.